AROUND
WESTBURY
IN OLD PHOTOGRAPHS

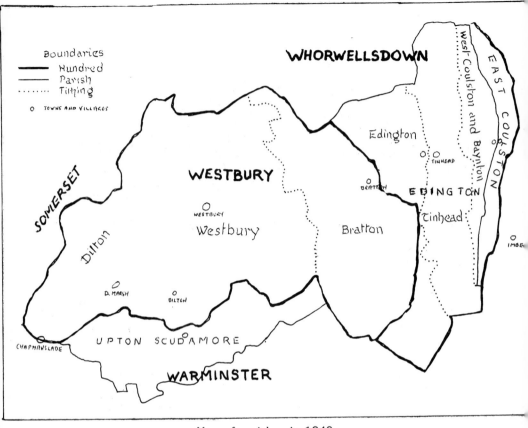

Map of parishes in 1840

Hundred, Parish and Tithing boundaries
that existed in the mid-nineteenth century.

AROUND
WESTBURY
IN OLD PHOTOGRAPHS

COMPILED BY
MICHAEL RANDALL

ALAN SUTTON
1989

Published in collaboration with
Wiltshire County Council
Library and Museum Service

Alan Sutton Publishing
Gloucester

First published 1989

British Library Cataloguing in Publication Data

Around Westbury in old photographs.
1. Wiltshire. Westbury, history
I. Randall, Michael, 1931–
942.3'15

ISBN 0-86299-625-2

Front Cover Illustration:
Imber sheep-shearing team in 1900.

Typesetting and origination by
Alan Sutton Publishing
Printed in Great Britain by
WBC Print Limited

CONTENTS

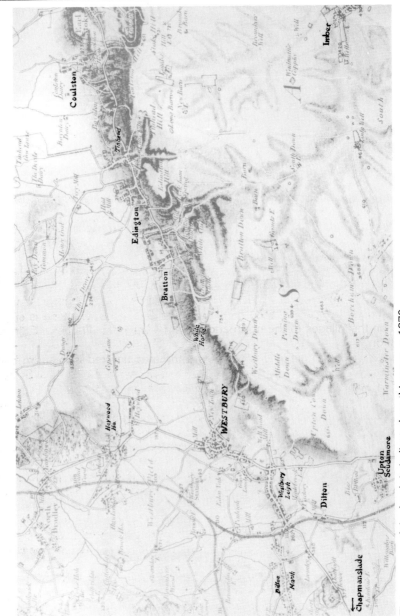

The coverage of the book is indicated on this map, c. 1870.

INTRODUCTION

After the egotistic satisfaction of seeing my name on the cover of a book and flattered by the kind letters that came after the publication of *Westbury in Old Photographs*, I fell an easy prey to the many requests to do another of the villages around. I also welcomed the opportunity to incorporate the corrections on Westbury which had helpfully been sent in.

Around Westbury in Old Photographs was to be the title and the area allocated to me was from Coulston, through Westbury and on to Chapmanslade and Upton Scudamore. I requested that Imber be included as there is a strong local interest in this isolated village lost to its community since 1943. Only Chitterne is slightly closer than the villages to the north and there are links with Coulston, Edington and Bratton.

The title is not geometrically accurate as the area covered is far from being circular but 'Astride Westbury' lacks elegance and 'Below the North West Scarp of Salisbury Plain with occasional Excursions' is hardly succinct.

It soon became apparent that the supply of old photographs has no rules and is not proportioned to one's needs. It is like prospecting for gold, an occasional nugget is turned up and sometimes a vein alongside makes one rich beyond measure. Laborious 'mining' can then yield nothing though you know there must be more. It takes little more than a cursory glance at the relative size of sections to see where I have 'struck gold'. To make things worse, imagine how painful it is to have to discard some nuggets when at the end all has to fit into a compartmental container of fixed size!

I rapidly found too that it is one thing to fossick around a town where one had lived for more than a decade but totally another to barge into a close-knit village community where families have lived for generations, even centuries. One village, dare I say it, I had not previously even visited.

Having scuttled my credentials, I hope the objectivity with which the book is written has its advantages and will succeed in reminding some people of the scenes of their youth and others of the continuum of which they are now a part. If nothing else, these pictures now have a better chance of living on for future generations to enjoy.

The strand running through the region was a woollen one, for sheep dominated the economy from the rearing of them to the manufacture of cloth, through all its processes. It is fitting then that the cover picture should be of a team of shearers and pleasing that they come from the 'lost' village of Imber.

Rates of pay in years gone by mean little on their own, unless one can relate them to buying power and so convert them to today's values. That I cannot do with the scale of pay for shepherds in 1655 given below but fortunately the pay for certain tradesmen, also in Wiltshire, at that date is known, so there is some measure of relativity.

The source document gives a weekly wage for the tradesmen which varies with the season (more in the summer, 'Annunciation to Michaelmas') and is roughly halved if 'meate and drink' is supplied. The shepherd's pay is given as an annual figure so I have calculated the tradesman's as an annual sum too, using the 'without meate and drinke' rate.

These are the tradesmen listed at the same rate: master carpenter, bricklayer, plumber, glazier, joiner, millwright, wheelwright and plasterer.

	Annual pay in 1655
Tradesmen	not above £2 18s. 6d.
Common Shepherd under 21	not above £2 0s. 0d.
Common Shepherd over 21	not above £3 0s. 0d.
Shepherd keeping 600 sheep	not above £3 6s. 8d.
Chief Shepherd keeping 5,000 sheep and above	not above £5 0s. 0d.

Now we are ready to start on our travels and there are some lovely villages on our way. We will start at Coulston, where a murdered child lies buried, on to the Plain to the deserted village of Imber and back down the old slow coach road to Tinhead. Edington with its splendid monastic church from where a bishop was dragged and beaten to death, is close by and up the Milbourne we reach the mills' sites and the church, isolated since the Black Death, at Bratton. Passing the White Horse we take a revisionary stroll round Westbury and Westbury Leigh with Dilton Marsh lengthily extended beyond. The journey then takes us up to and over the Westbury–Frome Road to drop into a peaceful valley where Dilton nestles with its church exactly as it was 200 years ago. From Biss Bottom we climb to the ridge-top village of Upton Scudamore, 'Opetone' in the *Domesday Book*, from where Scudamore organs originated. The coach road north-west brings us to Dead Maid's Corner and we finish with an all too short look at Chapmanslade strung out along the Frome road to the Somerset border.

SECTION ONE

Coulston

To start our walk we must find our first village, well hidden among the trees and the spurs running north from Salisbury Plain, here reaching out across the B3098 West Lavington–Westbury Road.

The parish of East Coulston ('Covelstone' in the Domesday Book) before 1934 was nowhere more than half a mile wide and 4½ miles from north to south. In 1783 there were only nine houses and the church.

West Coulston is no more separated from the East than the other disparate elements of the village but it lay in the parish of Edington. The logical step of combining the two was taken in 1934, doubling the area of the parish of East Coulston. The discreet signpost off the B3078 drops the 'East', as have I, though on the map it remains.

The north of the parish is flat meadowland rising sharply to the south up the, now well-wooded, edge of the Plain to over 700 ft on Coulston Hill where there are isolated downland farms on the periphery of the military training area.

The church of St Andrew, later to be dedicated to St Thomas à Becket, is first mentioned in 1214 but parts of the building are from the previous century. Nonconformists were directionally orientated in the mid-nineteenth century, Methodists and Baptists meeting in cottages in East and West Coulston respectively. A chapel was built in 1872 but closed in 1937.

Schooling in the village began in 1808 with an old lady teaching about ten children for twopence per person per week. A day school was instituted for girls in 1819 though the curate was of the opinion that 'the poor were not desirous of education'! Simon Watson-Taylor built a school in 1855 with a home for the master but it closed in 1899 to become the village hall.

There are both grand and interesting houses, the earliest probably dating from the early seventeenth century.

The outside world became aware of this small hidden village after the wide publicity given to the murder of the 3-year-old boy, Francis Savill Kent, at Rode Hill House in 1860. The Kent family had lived at Baynton House just before Mr Kent's first wife died. She was buried in the churchyard and the murdered boy, son of his second wife, was interred in the same grave. The murder inquiry got nowhere but five years later one of the boy's stepsisters, Constance, aged 16 at the time of the murder, confessed and was imprisoned for 21 years. Several books have since been written on the affair and the inept investigations which followed the murder.

LOOKING NORTH from Coulston Hill over East Coulston, July 1989. Baynton House is visible in the centre.

WEST COULSTON from above Upper Baynton Farm, August 1989.

ST THOMAS À BECKET CHURCH was dedicated to St Andrew around 1500 but changed its allegiance in the late eighteenth century. The grave to the left of the picture is that of Mary Kent, first wife of S. Savill Kent Esq., then of Baynton House, and also of 3-year-old Francis Savill Kent, a son by his second wife, murdered at Road (Rode) Hill House in 1860. Constance Kent, the boy's stepsister, confessed to the crime five years later and was imprisoned for 21 years.

INTERIOR, 1889. A church in East Coulston was first mentioned in 1214 but a doorway dates from the late twelfth century.

A FAMILY IN SUNDAY BEST outside their thatched cottage in the 1880s.

BRICKFIELD FARM in 1907, farmed by Mr Dunford (to left of horse). A Miss Smith is on the left of the picture. Mr Dick Hale, now living in Edington, took over the farm from Mr Dunford. A field to the east of the farm was called Brickfield in 1840, the farmhouse being built later in the century. Mr Dunford was the last to make bricks.

CHILDREN DANCING ROUND THE MAYPOLE in 1922 on the lawn by the south end of Baynton House, to where Mr Kent and his family moved in 1852, weeks before his wife died.

THE STONE-BUILT GEORGIAN COULSTON HOUSE is the venue for this gathering of the Whitsun Club. People paid in throughout the year for a Whitsuntide 'spree'.

THE VILLAGERS assembled for Queen Victoria's Golden Jubilee celebrations in 1887. The population in 1871 was 133 so it looks to be a good turn-out...

...AND AGAIN for the Diamond Jubilee ten years later. The decorated barn is at Paget's Farm. Mr Perrett, farmer, is wearing a white bowler and the boy in the wide-brimmed hat in the second row is E.G. Hale who can be seen, grown up, on p. 18.

IN 1900, Jacob and Maria Pepler (on the right) celebrated 68 years of marriage. Jacob, 88, is wearing a smock made by his wife, almost as old, 'without the use of glasses'. The local paper went on: 'grand children and great grandchildren are fairly numerous'! Of their ten children, only four were surviving in 1900. Miss Drew and Mr & Mrs John Drew (on the left) were neighbours in the left half of the cottage.

WEST COULSTON, with Rose Cottage in the centre. The cottage was converted from a barn by Mr Pepler's father.

DITCHING TEAM. Left to right: Messrs Harrow (father of 'Bolo' – see p. 20), Miles and Early. Before the First World War, competitions were held.

MILKERS AT UPPER BAYNTON FARM in 1909. Left to right: H. Bathard, W. Lewis, G. Oram, C. Early.

REAPERS, 1885.

PETER JONES, a carter at Stokes March Farm, 1925.

HARVESTING, 1914.

SHEEP-SHEARING at Coulston House Farm. E.G. Hale, father of Mr Dick Hale, is fourth from left and Jim Early, fifth.

COULSTON UNITED FOOTBALL CLUB existed despite the small population. The team of 1912–13. Back row, left to right: Harry Burgess, Reg Burgess (nephew), Alf Sadd, -?-, Tom Ronchetti (butler at Baynton House). Middle row: -?-, -?-, -?-. Front row: Cantello (died WWI), -?-, Bill Harrow (died WWI), Minus (died WWI), Orchard.

A 'WELCOME HOME' PARTY for those returning from the Second World War. Left to right: P. Hale, H. Wheeler, Jim Smith, Jack -?-, Tom Smith, -?- Fennel, -?- Richards and -?- Atkins (brothers-in-law). Colonel Anderson is on the right.

A MARVELLOUS STUDY of costume in 1887. Although it is just out of the area of the book, outside Erlestoke Church, the boy standing by the donkey is 'Bolo' Harrow, a Coulston boy who joined the Metropolitan Police (F Division), returning to Coulston on retirement. Victoria Watson-Taylor is in the trap. Her family owned most of the land for miles around.

THE BELL INN ceased to be a pub in 1955.

Imber

It may seem strange that having just begun our wander round the north-west fringe of Salisbury Plain, we immediately divert to Imber. Tidier it would have been to start there and circuit anti-clockwise but I baulked at dropping my readers in the middle of nowhere without warning, for Imber is not as other places!

Instead we will take the lane south from East Coulston by Flinty Knapp, climbing to over 700 ft above sea level, and join the old slow coach route from Tinhead. On reaching the Lavington–Tilshead road we read the warning to would-be highwaymen at St Joan à Gore's Cross. I am surprised they persisted in the area, for in 1716 in different locations, two robbers were shot by local farmers on the same day. They are buried in Imber churchyard.

All the tracks across the Plain were marked by heaps of chalk, for it is very easy to lose your way (I know!) and the only road was from Warminster, completed in the 1890s. A bus and carrier service was not set up until after the First World War. We will take the now metalled road westwards, which drops down into the secluded little valley with Imber nestling in it astride the boundary between the hundreds of Rowborough Regis and Heytesbury. All writers on Imber variously quote, or misquote, the couplet, 'Imber on the Down, Four/five/seven miles from any town.' Certainly Warminster, a town, is seven miles and the nearest village is four miles, so take your pick.

The population of 'Imemerie' (Domesday Book spelling) was under 50 in 1086, rising to a maximum of 510 in 1840, reducing to 152 in 1931, then with six weeks' notice in 1943 it dropped to nil when the inhabitants were moved out for the US army to carry out intensive pre-D-Day training. The promise that they could return after the fall of France was not honoured – not that much was left to return to. The military presence had been steadily encroaching, as the introduction of the rifle and change in tactics from the close order battle drills necessitated training areas. At the turn of the century 43,000 acres of Salisbury Plain were bought. During the First World War long-range guns fired over the village and some damage was done. Villagers were allowed out only three times a week to shop in Warminster. Afterwards the War Office continued to buy land and between 1928 and 1932 all the freehold in and around the village was purchased except for the church, school, chapel and The Bell Inn.

Now the 'village' is tidy with specially-built 'houses' for training while the church and a few remaining pre-war houses are poignant reminders of the lost community. My first visit was as a young soldier in the winter of 1950 as sleet-soaked night was falling. The dense undergrowth, piles or rubble and stark buildings presented a dismal scene. As I crouched in the modicum of shelter provided by the shell of Imber Court I wondered about those who had lived there, little thinking I would write about them 39 years later.

ONLY THE CHURCH would be recognizable to a previous inhabitant of Imber in this view taken on 2 September 1989. The 'houses', while lacking architectural merit, were built by the Ministry of Defence to provide the necessary facility for internal security training.

IMBER as it was before the war, looking up Church Road. The road disappearing behind the trees, on the right, passes the vicarage and becomes Carrion Pit Road.

ST GILES' CHURCH, from a tinted postcard of the 1920s. The nave is late thirteenth century and the tower is late fourteenth century. The chancel was rebuilt in 1849 by the patron, Lord Bath.

INTERIOR OF CHURCH in 1894 showing the fourteenth-century Rous effigies, vandalized in 1945 but now safe in Edington church. One bell also went there.

AS NOW, this picture I took in the 1960s shows the church fenced off and out of bounds to troops. The fabric is maintained by the Ministry of Defence. Of the furnishings removed, the pulpit went to Winterbourne Earls and the font to Brixton Deverill.

CHURCH ROAD leads off to the left from behind the lines of washing. What appears to be a large building on the horizon is a mystery I have been unable to solve.

THIS HOUSE is on the corner of Church Road, which goes over the bridge to the right.

VIEW FROM THE CHURCHYARD with the vicarage on the left, Parsonage Farm in the centre and the Church of England school in the right foreground.

FROM THE RIGHT of the top picture, this photograph presents the sorry sight of the village in 1945, after the US forces had used it for realistic street-fighting training. The council houses of the '30s are still recognizable as such and the vicarage looks remarkably unscathed, though it has since totally disappeared.

SCHOOLGIRLS of the 1890s, I would think.

ONE OF THE FEW BUILDINGS north of the 'main' road. The Post Office was built early this century. There was a 'Postman's Path' from Codford which joined Bungey's Lane (see p. 30), on which the postman would walk to deliver the mail in the morning, taking the outgoing letters with him in the afternoon.

COTTAGES OPPOSITE IMBER COURT with The Bell Inn beyond. Further on from the pub lay the Dring and here lived the last dewpond makers, four of whom were still working until they were nearly 80.

AN EARLY PICTURE of the same cottages with a delightful group of inhabitants, complete with Victorian perambulator.

IMBER COURT, the eighteenth-century manor house of Imber, as it was before 1920. In the early nineteenth century the house was used as a boys' boarding school.

THIS IS NOT THE RESULT of the Army's use of Imber but of a fire in 1921 which gutted the building.

THE HOUSE WAS REBUILT after the fire and the style altered with a re-designed gabled roof.

YET ANOTHER ROOF STYLE – the shuttered, truncated Imber Court of 1989. The re-roofed remains of The Bell Inn can be seen in the centre of the picture.

SEAGRAM'S FARM (East Farm), built in 1880 at the eastern edge of the village, where Mrs Archer-Smith (then Molly Dean) lived.

INTACT BUT DILAPIDATED, Seagram's Farm in 1948. The single-storey wing was a later addition to the house. The building still survives. Leading off to the right is the 'American Road' to Heytesbury, so named since the US army improved it in 1944. It was previously known as Bungey's Lane, from the name of a farmer's dog whose skin was preserved as a butter container!

IMBER lies hidden in a steep-sided valley with the Warminster–Lavington road running through the village alongside the stream. Flash-floods can easily occur as here in 1911. The building on the left, once The Nag's Head, still stands (with four of its eight chimneys remaining). Seagram's Farm is straight ahead.

THE SMITHY AND TINKER'S FARM are to the right of the picture. The small stream runs alongside the 'main' road.

DON NASH, the village blacksmith, married Annie Pearce in 1914. Sydney Pearce, the shepherd, is seated on the right. Their son Cyril died in October 1989, aged 71, and the Imber churchyard was reopened so that he could be buried with other members of the family.

DON NASH'S SMITHY is on the right.

THRESHING AT IMBER. Left to right: W. Burges, S. Dean, -?- Pearce, J. Marsh, W. Pearce. Standing below the elevator: H. Marsh, and the boy, Reg Marden.

THRESHING in the 1920s with a different engine and machine.

ABOVE: on the right, Mrs Archer-Smith (nee Dean), looks at some of the photographs for this book of her home village, outside Imber church before the annual service on 2 September 1989.

RIGHT: an earlier member of the Dean family from Imber suffered at the hands of highwaymen in 1839, commemorated by this stone at St Joan à Gore's Cross.

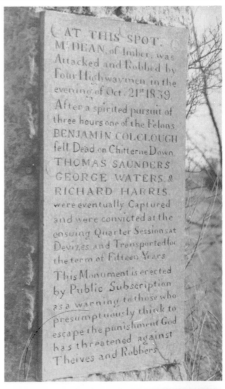

THE END COTTAGE in Church Road.

Tinhead

Before the take-over of the Plain for military training you could have taken a more direct route back from Imber on tracks past Brounckers Well, up the valley to the west of Coulston Down and over Tinhead Hill to join up again with the old coach route at the tumulus near the (still standing) ancient milestone (Bath 17, Sarum 19). This track leads us to Coach Hollow in Tinhead.

There is no Tinhead on my map, I hear you say. I know, and it is not on any signpost either. However, if you look at the Lamb Inn sign on the end of the building, there you will find Tinhead written. It is in fact part of the parish of Edington but it is geographically separate and I hope it will make better sense of the photographs by splitting Edington into two sections.

The name means 'ten hides' but Domesday throws no light on this holding. The first reference to it is in connection with a fine for some forest offence by Philip de Tunhede in 1190.

Most of the houses are on the road leading north from the Lamb Inn towards Steeple Ashton and on small roads off it. Beckett's House goes back to about 1600 and may have been the home of the Whitakers, wealthy clothiers at that period. The eighteenth-century, solid brick-built George Inn used to be a convenient 'pull in' for coaches before venturing up onto the exposed road over Salisbury Plain, en route for Salisbury. It recently ceased to be a pub.

An old malthouse was used as a place of worship in 1794, probably by Baptists, who were certainly using it in 1851 but it closed in 1897 when the lease expired. The Methodists too had lease problems, for after meeting in a cottage from about 1787, they made a chapel in an old coachhouse but were not allowed to renew the lease in 1827. After again meeting in a cottage for a short period, they built a chapel in Coach Hollow. It was enlarged in 1848 to seat a congregation of 360 and virtually rebuilt in 1904.

The northern low-lying land, in common with that around the other villages below the scarp, was mainly arable and meadows with the sheep pastures on the downs. Tinhead has only a tiny stream but there was a water-mill in the fourteenth-century. The village water supply came from springs. A limekiln stood on the hill above Tinhead through most of the nineteenth century.

The Chartists (working-class political reformers) held small meetings in Tinhead in 1838 and 1839 addressed by William Carrier from Trowbridge.

TINHEAD FROM EDINGTON HILL, linked to Edington only by the row of council houses on the left.

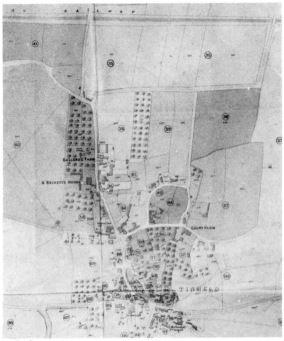

MAP OF TINHEAD, C. 1910.

HAYMAKING ON TINHEAD HILL. The carter on the left is Mr Burgess. William Drewett, who we meet again in Edington, is in the middle with a pitchfork. No farming scene is complete without the casks and jars of cider or beer.

BALANCE PLOUGH AND ENGINES on Tinhead Hill.

THE LOWER END OF COACH HOLLOW, south of the Westbury Road, with the Methodist chapel, first built in 1828, enlarged in 1848 and virtually rebuilt in 1904.

THE SMITHY, pre–1914.

WOMAN DRAWING WATER from the spring by Tinhead pond.

Village Pond and Pond House, Tinhead.

ANOTHER VIEW OF THE POND. Happily, an access road to a new property which would have meant filling in part of the pond, was prevented.

THE POND, LOOKING SOUTH. The girl is taking her bucket of water home. Even after mains water was brought to the village, some preferred to use the spring.

THE OLD SLOW COACH ROUTE from Bath came through Tinhead, before climbing up Coulston Hill to continue towards Salisbury, until the late eighteenth century. The coaches stopped at The George Inn, brick-built in the eighteenth century.

A LATER VIEW of The George Inn on Lower Road.

THE HUNT meets opposite The George in 1953.

THE SHOP, Court Lane, Tinhead, c. 1890. Nellie Swanborough, George Hascock (in the trap), son of Mr & Mrs George Hascock (on the right).

THE SHOP AT A LATER DATE. Thatch has given way to tiles.

TINHEAD STORES, 1935. Doug Reed, on the path, became owner of Castle Garage, Bratton.

GROUP OF VILLAGERS in a field by Little Court Lane.

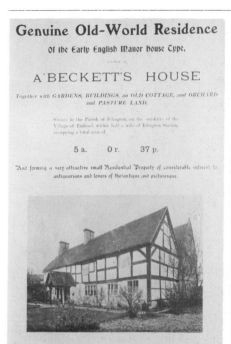

Genuine Old-World Residence

Of the Early English Manor House Type,

A'BECKETT'S HOUSE

Together with GARDENS, BUILDINGS, an OLD COTTAGE, and ORCHARD and PASTURE LAND,

Situate in the Parish of Edington, on the outskirts of the Village of Tinhead, within half a mile of Edington Station, occupying a total area of

5 a.   0 r.   37 p.

And forming a very attractive small Residential Property of considerable interest to antiquarians and lovers of the antique and picturesque.

FROM A 1910 CATALOGUE for the sale of part of the Erlestoke Estate. The house is of sixteenth-century origin.

MR H. BATHARD (left) with Charlie Hamm at Beckett's House Stables in 1902. The horse belonged to timber hauliers of Marlborough, working at the sawmill.

LADIES out for a drive.

SLADE'S FARM in the late 1880s with Mr and Mrs Hurle, grandparents of Mrs Bathard.

JASPER AMOR at his stables in Slade's Farm.

STEAM TRACTION ENGINE at Ballard's Farm in the 1930s. The driver is Jack Miles, with Jack Amor on the left. Sitting is William 'Stump' Osmond. Standing is George Drewett and George Pearce is on the right.

ELSIE BOULTER in 1902, in Long Hollow.

LONG HOLLOW, September 1933. Children queuing at the well for Mrs Bathard to fill the water bottles and dixies of troops of the 8th Infantry Brigade, on manoeuvres on Salisbury Plain.

SECTION FOUR

Edington

Much of the argument about whether the Wiltshire or Somerset Edington 'owned' Alfred's victory over the Danes in AD 878, stems from the derivation of the name. This is complicated by the fact that both are spelled 'Edendone' in the Domesday Book. The Anglo-Saxon Chronicle records this great battle, which led to the Treaty of Wedmore and the withdrawal of Guthram with his Danes from Wessex, in two sentences: 'He proceeded to Ethandun, and there fought with all the army and put them to flight, riding after them as far as the fortress, where he remained a fortnight. Then the army gave him hostages with many vows that they would go out of his kingdom!' Not a lot to go on! The belief that the original Westbury White Horse by Bratton Castle was cut by Alfred to commemorate this victory, makes the Bratton earthworks a likely starter for 'the fortress'.

The Revd William Creswell, in his book of 1910, arguing the Somerset case, blamed William Camden, the sixteenth-century antiquary 'who, without any real proof, gave it out as a certain and well assured fact that the Battle of Edington was fought in Wiltshire, an "idolon specus" – a preconceived fancy of his own'.

I don't think I will risk an 'idolon specus' but accept most modern historians' support for Camden, despite the White Horse red herring – if you take my meaning! Though there is a lack of photographs of the battle, some of the old postcards of Edington have a reference to Ethandun, so there is some relevance to this discussion of its authenticity.

Leaving Tinhead by the minor road running parallel to the Westbury road and north of it, a row of council houses is passed, the only housing link across the $\frac{1}{4}$-mile gap between Tinhead and Edington. The first building we come to, on the north-east corner of the village, is the magnificent fourteenth-century priory church, large enough to seat the total population of Edington and Tinhead with ease, I would think. It was built on the site of a late Norman church by William of Edington, Bishop of Winchester and Lord Treasurer and Chancellor of England in Edward III's reign. Edward's son, the Black Prince, had requested William to found a Priory for the Bonhommes, an Augustinian group of monks. It is probably the finest example of a monastic church in Wiltshire. Henry VIII closed the monastery in 1539.

Two local wealthy families were united in the fourteenth century when the daughter of Sir John Pavely of Broke, Lord of the Manor of Westbury, married Sir Ralph Cheney of Edington, and their tomb is in the nave of the church.

The supply of water from the Milbourne, which rises in Luccombe in Bratton, provided power for the setting up of mills for the woollen industry. A mill in Edington is first mentioned in the mid-fourteenth century.

The Edington Music Festival, held in the church in August every year, attracts visitors from all over the country and abroad.

The remainder of the village, with several houses of interest, is scattered around the spurs running north from the Plain.

EDINGTON FROM THE HILL, with the priory church on the right, August 1989.

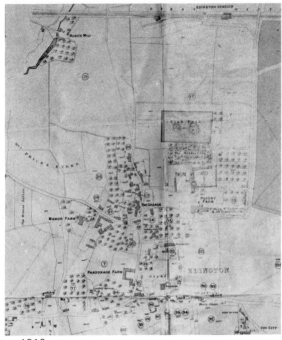

MAP OF EDINGTON, c. 1910.

AN EARLIER VIEW from the hill, probably *c.* 1910. The plume of smoke from the train indicates the main London route to the west via Westbury. The station is in the centre.

ANOTHER POSTCARD, from further east, postmarked 1912.

THE POST OFFICE among the small group of houses at the foot of the Downs, south of the Westbury Road. The name of the area was recorded as Little London in 1773 but by the 1880s it was known as the City.

WESTBURY ROAD in Edington, with the bakery and Berrett's shop on the right.

WHITE HORSE INN on the Westbury Road. The man standing, facing right, was killed in the First World War.

THE WHITE HORSE INN AGAIN. The horse and trap on the left belongs to Pidgeon Bros, butchers of Westbury.

CONDUIT COTTAGES (sometimes written as Cundick) on Westbury Road. The end house caught fire on New Year's Eve 1940 when a motor cycle was started under the eaves, setting the thatch alight. Attempts to put out the fire were hampered by the water freezing.

COTTAGES ON THE WESTBURY ROAD opposite the road to the church.

THE SAME ROAD JUNCTION as on the opposite page. The vicarage is prominent on the hill.

FROM THE WESTBURY ROAD, looking towards the priory church.

BEFORE REACHING THE CHURCH, The Plough was on the left. This card was postmarked 1912 and the licensee then was B. Pavy. It is now a private house.

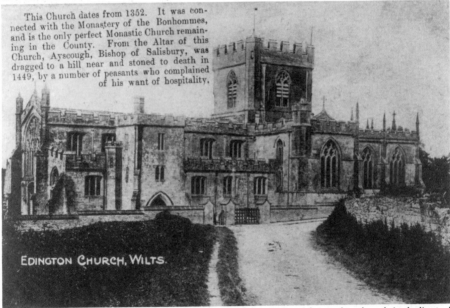

This Church dates from 1352. It was connected with the Monastery of the Bonhommes, and is the only perfect Monastic Church remaining in the County. From the Altar of this Church, Ayscough, Bishop of Salisbury, was dragged to a hill near and stoned to death in 1449, by a number of peasants who complained of his want of hospitality,

EDINGTON CHURCH, WILTS.

THIS POSTCARD of 1916 provides some information but it doesn't say the church is dedicated to St Mary the Virgin, St Katherine and All Saints; ample scope for patronal festivals! I thought Cade's Rebellion, when Bishop Aiscough was murdered, was in 1450 and he was killed because he spent too much time away at Court as confessor and secretary to Henry VI, but he may have been inhospitable to rebels too.

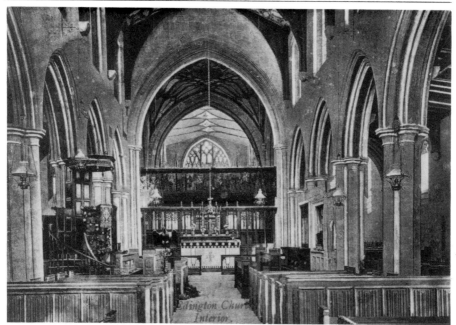

THIS BEAUTIFUL FOURTEENTH-CENTURY CHURCH is a good example of the transition to the Perpendicular style from the Decorated. The nave exhibits more of the former while the chancel has a more Decorated character. The screen is early sixteenth-century. This postcard was postmarked 1907.

THE 'PRIORY' AND CHURCH. The order of Bonhommes (sometimes written 'Bonshommes'), established here by Bishop Edington of Winchester in 1358, was one of two such establishments in England. They followed the rule of St Augustine. The 'Priory' House on the left is built on the original site.

FANCY DRESS COMPETITORS lead a procession out of the churchyard.

AN EARLIER GROUP pose for their photograph in 1895.

THE MONASTERY GARDENS were important to the social life of the village.

A WINDOW of the original priory building remains as a monument in the garden.

BOATING was popular on the lake.

AN INTERESTING LINE-UP OF CARS, with their uniformed chauffeurs, in Station Road by the Monastery Gardens, but for what occasion is not known.

MRS BURBIDGE in the uniform of the Women's Land Army, during the Second World War.

LADIES' DRESS OF 1902. Mrs Mark Maslin (née Drewett) standing outside Grange Cottage (Edington Cottage). This was the lower of the two before they were made into one.

OLD MANOR FARM COTTAGE in Lower Street, c. 1900, with Jacob Drewett, remembered for his rendering of the same song for 50 years at the annual pig club dinner! The man by the hedge is collecting water from the spring.

INMEAD, with Walt Collett and George Wheeler (in front of his farm) on motorbikes and Fred Wheeler (older brother of George) in the centre.

BUTCHER'S CART in Inmead Lane.

WILLIAM DREWETT was the village roadman, when not helping with the hay or harvest. On the left, he is with his lunch in its red spotted handkerchief and jar of cider at his feet. On the right is a tar boiler for re-surfacing the road.

WILLIAM DREWETT back to haymaking.

JASPER AMOR'S HORSE, Silver, the last working farm-horse in the area, who died in 1973 aged almost 30. Mr Amor bought him as a little colt at a fair; he was the best horse he ever had.

CHAIN HARROWING in the 1920s.

THREE EDINGTON BOYS, 1919. Herbert Maslin, and Jim and Ernie Newman.

MUCK CART, 1920s.

SHEEP-WASHING AT HUDD'S MILL, down by the railway, in 1912. Left to right: Jim Early (with pole), Ben Coleman (shepherd from Bratton with beer), behind him George Wheeler, Bill White in front of hurdle, Bill Wheeler and Annie Miles (with hat, behind boys), W. Price (Edington Farm), his sister Ann Price and Mrs Stewart from London. Doing the washing are the shepherd Frank Whatley and -?- Smith from Bratton.

THE NEW GWR LINE to the west via Westbury was built in 1900. Local labour must have been recuited as it progressed, for the father of the Newman boys on the previous page is on the platform of the steam shovel.

IT IS PRESUMED this is an open-air workshop for the building of the railway.

EDINGTON AND BRATTON RAILWAY STATION WITH STAFF. The poster on the left announces the change of the timetable when the Westbury route became the GWR's main route to Plymouth and the west in 1906. The location of the station favoured Edington rather more than Bratton.

A 'KING' CLASS LOCOMOTIVE in British Railway livery runs easily through Edington with its train of at least 12 coaches. HST 125 trains now use this line but there has been no station since 1952.

A MULTI-VIEW POSTCARD of Edington.

ANOTHER POSTCARD, produced during the First World War.

ONE OF THE MANY LOCAL MEN who served their country in the forces. J. Bathard served with the 6th Wilts and was killed in action on 26 September 1915.

SECTION FIVE

Bratton

We continue towards Westbury and, within a mile, drop down to the old mill stream (Milbourne or, in later years, the Bratt), and Bratton rises steeply before you. It is a lovely village with many interesting and fine buildings. Roman burials and the site of a villa indicate early settlement. The village appears tidily compact, with little of the usual fringe development, and it comes as a surprise to find it is made up from three separate settlements dating back to before the fourteenth century and identifiably separate until comparatively recent times. The gap between two has been filled by twentieth-century development and the orchards, which were interspersed between houses along Melbourne Street, have been covered by houses. The remoteness and isolation of the church is puzzling until it is realized this was the centre of the third community, which was deserted after most of the inhabitants died of the Black Death in 1348.

So, round the church was Stoke, or Little Stoke, and across the valley along the mill stream and up Melbourne Street to the top of the hill, was Milbourne. Bratton itself was centred on the Court House and the old Manor House, the foundations of which are thought to be nearby.

Bratton was a chapelry of the ancient parish of Westbury until 1845 when the eastern portion of nearly 4,000 acres was assigned to the church as the parish of Bratton. The civil parish of Bratton was not created until 1894.

Nonconformity gained a hold in the village in the late seventeenth and early eighteenth centuries when preachers came from Erlestoke and Westbury Leigh. The Whitaker family provided a meeting place for the Baptists from 1720 and has given active support since, as also later did the Pococks and Reeves, among others.

One cannot dip into Bratton, as I am doing, without rapidly realizing that the names of Whitaker and Reeves are rooted firmly in its history. Their story and the history of Bratton has been published in books separately by historians Marjorie Reeves and Jean Morrison. I must beg their forbearance for my superficial, though I hope not misleading, selection of facts and events. As it is, Bratton has the lion's share of the book.

So let us explore the village: farming, the final demise of the woollen industry and the skills, both traditional and modern, brought together in a versatile agricultural engineering business. I hope you will then want to know more and read the books.

BRATTON FROM THE HILL, August 1989.

FROM THE HILL in 1901. The church is on the left and The Elms, the home of the Reeves, is prominent in the middle foreground, with works of Messrs R. & J. Reeves at 11 o'clock to the house.

Bratton. There was once a camp here and it is thought to have been the entrenchment to which Guthrum the Dane retired after he was defeated by Alfred in 878 at Edington.

THIS WINTER VIEW gives a clearer view of Bratton, 1914.

GREETINGS FROM BRATTON WILTS

A DECORATIVE POSTCARD from the early 1900s. The thatched cottages in the bottom right picture were in Melbourne Street. In the farm opposite, a man leaned too heavily on a damp mud and wattle dividing wall, and fell through!

BRATTON.

There is a tradition that at the battle of Ethandune in 878 the Danes were posted in the little valley under the hill.

DROPPING DOWN INTO BRATTON from Edington, Westbury Road becomes Melbourne Street. The mill stream flowing under the road from Stradbrook was known as the Milbourne in the Middle Ages. Lower Road goes off to the right and Stradbrook to the left. Bratton House is prominent at the top of the hill. The legend of the Danes in the valley may have arisen from the name Danes Lye which in fact means 'Valley clearing'.

STRADBROOK, BRATTON

THE CHURCH PATH leads off to the left. In the centre the path with steps down the hill called The Ball, emerges to the right of the cottages. Behind the horse and cart is the Wesleyan chapel with baptismal steps opposite, leading down to the stream. Stradbrook Mill on the right was owned by Mr George Brent of Luccombe but it closed in 1891 and he died in 1900.

J. MERRITT, the builder, demolished the mill chimney in 1909, having gained experience 13 years before with Mill Vale chimney.

THE SON OF GEORGE BRENT built three cottages, Cleeve Terrace, on the site of the mill, as can be seen on the right of the picture.

BEFORE THE DUST HAD SETTLED, the workmen and spectators posed for a souvenir photograph. The 6 hp low pressure beam engine is partly visible through the dust. The mill had been used for scribbling and then spinning before its closure.

ANOTHER VIEW of Stradbrook showing Cleeve Terrace more clearly. A smithy was also situated in Stradbrook.

SHEEP-WASHING before 1909 (as Stradbrook Mill is still standing). The steps used for baptisms can be seen below the chapel. The sheep here seem unwilling 'converts'!

WHETHER THE CASKS are for the refreshment of the men or medication for the sheep is not clear but precedent suggests the former. Mr Frank Whatley, standing in the water, as we earlier saw him at Hudd's Mill, was the youngest of 15. He went to work with his father on Grants Farm as a shepherd's boy at the age of 12 in 1869, earning half a crown a week. His wide range of skills were still in demand when he was in his 70s and he was widely known and respected as 'Farmer' Whatley. c. 1905.

AN ACTION SHOT OF THE WASHING.

A NINETEENTH-CENTURY PHOTOGRAPH (possibly the only photograph) of Luccombe Mill. The land was leased from Lord Bath in 1809 and the mill and house built by Thomas Jarvis, then rented by Isaac, Samuel and George Brent in turn. The mill had an overshot water-wheel with a 15 ft fall of water available, and by 1847 had a steam engine.

THE ORNAMENTAL MILL-POND by Luccombe House.

THE HOUSE AND POND remained after the mill was demolished. The house has here lost the small gable in the centre.

COMBE VALLEY.

LOOKING BACK past Luccombe House to Stradbrook and beyond.

THE REVERSE VIEW OF THE TOP PICTURE. Two traction engines are tackling White Cleeves earlier than 1905.

LUCCOMBE ROAD becomes Imber Road as it climbs onto the Downs.

IMBER ROAD winding up towards South Down Farm. The combe on the right was known as Happy Valley.

Bratton Church, Wilts.

THE DELIGHTFUL MINIATURE MEDIEVAL CHURCH OF ST JAMES now stands alone on the wooded hill below the Downs where the settlement of Stoke, or Little Stoke, used to be. The church was built on a Norman ground-plan and the font is Norman. Jacobean benches in the chancel came from Imber church.

THE CHURCH PATH FROM STRADBROOK is now a road.

Bratton Church & Steps. – This Church in the early English style was restored in 1680 and will seat 230 persons. There are two hundred and six steps leading to it.

EITHER PEOPLE CAN'T COUNT or somebody keeps changing the number of steps. Area guides modestly claim 180. On this tinted postcard of 1906 it is 206 and a study by young ordinands made it 208. I did not risk counting them!

I DOUBT if Charles Poffley risked the steps with his ice cream hand cart, or else the Walls ice cream tricycle slogan might have been modified to 'Stop me – if you can – and buy one'!

THE SETTING OF THE CHURCH is well illustrated here in the picture of Mr and Mrs Herbert Mead with horse, pig and chickens. They were smallholders of Milditch (otherwise known as Gooseberry or Pig Lane).

HAVING SEEN HOW REMOTE the church is from the village, this trench to lay a gas pipe must have been a long one.

A JOB WELL DONE.

THE SIX BELLS OF ST JAMES were cast in 1587, 1617, 1793, 1858 and 1897. They were re-tuned and re-hung in 1834 when the Revd Seymour Collett was vicar. Others known to be in the picture are Mr & Mrs L. Tinnams, Mrs P. Chapman, Miss E. Lawrence, Miss M. Smith, Mr G. Mead and Mr F. Emm.

A YEAR after Mr Merritt demolished the Stradbrook Mill and chimney, he is building the Bratton Church Institute, aided here by the Bishop laying the foundation stone, 1910.

THE POST OFFICE opposite the War Memorial and Bratton House. Patcombe Farm, now demolished, is further down with the dark roof and two chimneys. Belbin's bakery shop is to the left beyond the trees.

BRATTON HOUSE, prominent on the high ground off Melbourne Street is a stone-faced eighteenth-century building, home of the Ballard family until the nineteenth century.

THE BAPTIST MINISTER in Erlestoke preached in Bratton in 1720 in the house of Jeffery and Catherine Whitaker. The services moved to a schoolroom provided by Jeffery Whitaker until the present site of the chapel, Brown's Plot, was given in 1733 and the original chapel built in 1734, paid for by voluntary subscription. Though enlarged and restored, the building has retained its character.

BURY COTTAGES, c. 1915.

AT SOME UNKNOWN DATE, the Duke Inn was acquired by the church, but was sold in 1887 for £1,300. The inn sign does not look much like a Duke to me though what is visible could be his galloping charger (or a rocking horse, or pregnant duck)!

NO DOUBT that this is the Duke but it is next door to where the other building had stood. The name of the landlord on the sign appears to be William E. Standing but the last four letters are not clear.

Whale's Jaws, Duke Inn. Tea Gardens, Bratton.

I REMEMBER SEEING A PUB, before the war, on the Southend arterial Road, called The Whalebone Inn, with an arch of such bones. They seemed strange there but even more so in tea gardens in rural Wiltshire!

ANOTHER POSSESSION of the Duke Inn was this holiday chalet on the slopes of the Downs.

APPROACHING BRATTON from the north by Court Lane.

THE COURT HOUSE, an attractive timber-framed house, evolved from a single-storey fifteenth-century building incorporated into the largely seventeenth-century structure. At some stage the house was divided into several cottages. The original hamlet of Bratton had its centre here and a site nearby is thought to be that of the medieval manor house.

COTTAGES IN LOWER (NOW MILL) STREET.

SEVENTEENTH-CENTURY EMM'S FARM.

At Bratton in the County of Wilts.
are taught.

Writing in all hands Practical and Ornamental.

Arithmetick Vulgar and Decimal.

Geometry Superficial and Solid.

Trigonometry Plain and Spherical.

With the Application thereof to Surveying of Land Gauging Navigation &c.

Also Merchants Acco.ts

Jeffery Whitaker

July 30. 1750.

A BEAUTIFULLY WRITTEN PROSPECTUS for the teaching skills of Jeffery Whitaker in 1750. He lived from 1703 to 1775.

JOHN SAFFERY WHITAKER, born 1840, died 1915, here photographed c. 1900. He farmed Grant's Farm, one of the large farms on the Downs, south of the village.

THE YEW TREES IN LOWER ROAD. The early eighteenth-century house of the Whitaker family. A boys' boarding school was run in the house throughout most of the century from 1718.

PLOUGHING WITH OXEN on Grant's Farm. William Grant and son are guiding the plough. However the name of the farm came from Thomas Graunt in 1588.

SHEEP-SHEARING ON GRANT'S FARM. About one third of Bratton's farmland was lost when the Salisbury Plain training area was extended by purchase between 1928 and 1932 and sheep could not be kept on the hills.

A TEAM PULLS A REAPER-BINDER. The sheaves have yet to be stooked by hand. Fields of stooks were a lovely sight.

TRACTION ENGINE-POWERED THRESHING MACHINE at work on Grant's Farm. These machines went from farm to farm.

FAMILY PICNIC AT GRANT'S FARM.

PICNIC PARTY OUTSIDE BARN.

TURKEY-REARING.

CHILDREN AT GRANT'S FARM. Notice the barn standing on staddle-stones to prevent rats getting in.

A BARN on Scott's Farm, Bratton.

PAGEANT by the junior section of the Bratton Branch of the League of Nations, 1926.

THE OPENING OF THE CHEVERILL BAPTIST CHAPEL IN 1906. Left to right: J.S. Whitaker Esq. JP., Revd Charles Hobbs, Alfred Pocock Esq. (who lived at Melbourne House and gave the site for the chapel), Henry Reeves Esq. JP.

ROBERT REEVES, son of Henry, married Edith Sarah Whitaker, daughter of John Whitaker, in 1900. Nelson Reeves was the best man and Whitaker Coombes (killed in the First World War) the page. Bridesmaids: Jane Whitaker, Magdelene Coombes, Dorothy Coombes and Ethel Reeves. 'The Elms' was built for the couple on their marriage and remained the Reeves family home until 1989.

THE RIFLE CLUB was formed in 1862 and held monthly meetings on the range on the hill above the church. Robert Reeves is standing in the centre, wearing a light suit.

MEN OF BRATTON AND EDINGTON about to set off to enlist at the beginning of the First World War. The driver of the first car is Oswald Reeves. Mrs Scull is wishing them well and Nelson Reeves is stepping forward to ask her not to block the photographer's view, but the moment had been captured for posterity.

R. & J. REEVES & SON LTD. WORKS in Melbourne Street next to The Duke.

THE WORKS from the other end, with the blacksmith's shop in the foreground.

BRATTON FIRE ENGINE (now in Toronto Science Museum). Manned here by, back row: William Humphries, William Cook, Walter Smith, Leslie Tinnams, Ernest Auberton. Front row: George Smith, Fred Emm, H.G. Smith, Frank Barnes.

THE TOP YARD of Reeves before 1958. The shed on the right housed the fire engine. The sign by the petrol pumps does not say how much petrol you get for 1s. Now 5p buys about 1/5th of a pint (or 115 ml if you prefer). Doug Reed established his Castle Garage here when the works closed.

WORKERS AT REEVES.

IN THE BLACKSMITH'S SHOP, 1953. C. Lawrence operating the electric power hammer and George Chapman, who had worked at Reeves since 1919, at the anvil. In the background are W. Shibley, apprentice Victor Eyers and W. Cook aged 73, who had 54 years' service with the firm.

THE LAST WHEEL to be bonded at Reeves, 1957. The hot bond (iron tyre) is fitted over the wooden wheel for it to shrink tightly on to it. Lionel Francis, Ivor Smith and Walter Shibley are the craftsmen.

PRODUCTS OF R. & J. REEVES & SON LTD, in front of the erecting shop. The elevator, in here for overhaul, was based on their successful design in the 1890s. Light seed drills are in the foreground. Miss Kathleen Reeves, of The Elms, remained Director and Secretary of the company until its closure in 1970. It became a private limited company in 1902.

A FAMILY outside their cottage in Melbourne Street.

BEN COLEMAN, shepherd.

MR AND MRS A.A. POFFLEY AND RELATIONS set off on their motorcycles.

MR & MRS AMBROSE MATTHEWS.

MARY REEVES, a poet. Her brother, Eli, was a basket-weaver.

JAMES NEWMAN, a carter, outside the Court House.

ROSE SMITH, who lived in Burbage Cottage, Milditch.

Westbury White Horse. This picturesque memorial of Alfred the Great's decisive victory over the Danes at Ethandunes (Edington) A.D. 878, is situated about two miles from the town of Westbury. It was formed by stripping the turf from the chalk downs on the northern slope of Salisbury Plain. The extreme length of the Horse from head to tail, both included 175 feet. Height from feet to shoulder, 107 feet. Circumference of eye, 25 feet.

SINCE BRATTON became a parish in its own right, the White Horse on Bratton Down lies within Bratton Parish boundary, though is not visible from the village. The horse was re-cut in 1778 over a smaller one facing the other way but there is no evidence to indicate any earlier date than 1700, despite the claim on the card. It became a 'Dark' Horse during the Second World War to prevent it aiding the navigation of German aircraft.

THE NEW LONDON-WESTBURY LINE being built from Patney & Chirton in 1900 is here being cut past Bratton. It was opened as a through route in 1906, reducing the time of the 'Cornish Riviera Limited' to Plymouth by 20 minutes to 4 hrs 10 mins. The time was further reduced to 4 hrs in 1927 when the 'King' class locomotives were introduced.

SECTION SIX

Westbury

The 'high road' over the White Horse or the 'low road' from Bratton past the cemetery will bring you to Westbury. This will be a familiar stamping ground to those who vicariously trudged the length and breadth of the town through the pages of my Westbury in Old Photographs, published in 1988. I will not, therefore, 'stamp' over it again but drop in here and there where either there is another picture to show or a correction to be made. The earlier book will henceforth be referred to as 'Vol 1' for the sake of brevity.

First I must disentangle a muddle over chapels, the explanation of which is too lengthy for a caption. In 1662, the Vicar of All Saints, Philip Hunton, was removed from his living. He then held house meetings out of which the Congregational church grew. A chapel was built on the east side of Warminster Road, opposite Leigh (then known as 'Lower') Road. Thus it was called the Lower Meeting. The chapel was rebuilt in its present form in 1821 and is now the United Reform Church.

When the Minister in 1751 dared to preach against slavery, some of the congregation withdrew to form a second church. They opened a church on the west side of the road in 1763 called the Top, or Upper, Meeting, as the area was known as Top o' the Town. Thus the original chapel became the Old Lower Meeting, Old Independent Meeting or Old Congregational Chapel (though in its rebuilt form it was, and looked, newer than the other). In altitude too, the 'Lower' is considerably higher than the 'Upper', as an aid to confusion. The two did not join up again until 1940 when the 'Upper' was closed.

I had done pretty well, I thought, to sort my uppers from my lowers but then in Vol. 1, p. 107, put my foot in it by muddling the Wesleyan Chapel/Masonic Hall into the mix. This chapel is quite separate and is off the Warminster Road opposite the junction with Haynes Road. My apologies all round.

All 'champions of traditional rural England' look for and see the black side and the arch champion, William Cobbett, didn't pull his punches in 1826 when he visited Westbury. A 'nasty, odious rotten borough, a really rotten place', he described it, and the mills he thought were 'ready to tumble down, as well as many of the houses'. Mind you, it was a very difficult time with much unemployment and low wages.

A pride and interest in our home town will prevent it becoming 'a really rotten place' again. It was pleasing to read in the local press in recent months, a call for the setting up of a Westbury History Society. Perhaps books such as these, prime the pump of interest. Thus encouraged, on we go.

SPREAD OUT ALONG THE DOWNS, 20–30,000 sheep assembled for the annual sheep fair in September must have been quite a sight and the importance of them to the area without dispute.

THE WHITE HORSE, WESTBURY.

FRANK WHATLEY, the shepherd from Bratton, claimed that when he was 19 he wondered whether he could pen a flock of sheep on the White Horse. With the aid of a good dog, he succeeded in rounding up 630 sheep on the body with none on the grass. What a pity no photographer was there!

A FINE VIEW of the Iron Age earthworks of Bratton Castle and the White Horse, which was not cut by Alfred to commemorate his victory over the Danes in 878, as popular local lore would have it. Planners continue to apply for permission to develop further beyond Newtown and the lower slopes of the White Horse. I trust they will continue to be turned down.

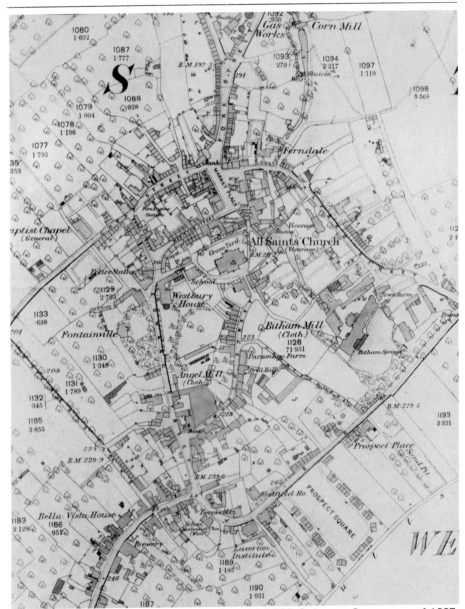

THIS SECTION from a much-folded and yellowed 1:2,500 Ordnance Survey map of 1887, shows a great deal of interesting detail. It is here printed at approximately 13 in to a mile.

THE CEMETERY lies below the White Horse alongside the road from Bratton.

BRATTON ROAD comes in from the left past the thatched barn. The Church of England Day School is on the corner opposite Alfred Street and Newtown goes on up past the school towards the White Horse. The barn has now gone and the school is a pottery.

FROM THE JUNCTION of Leigh (Lower) Road and Warminster Road, looking east. In Vol. 1, p. 103, Dr Trevor Shorland (uncle by marriage to Mr G.W.W. Laverton) was pictured in front of the trees on the right but his name was wrongly spelled. The last house visible is 'Bella Vista' not 'The Vineyards' (Vol. 1, p. 102). Bella Vista was also a school, founded by Mrs Catherine Jefferies, wife of Mr Jip Jefferies, organist at All Saints.

THESE TWO PHOTOGRAPHS, (much cleaned up copies of copies) are claimed to have been taken as early as the 1850s by R.R. Taylor. Abraham Wilkins, the forbidding-looking Sunday School Superintendent on the right, died in 1865 so we know the picture must be earlier than that! The Old Congregational Chapel (Old Independent or Lower Meeting) however, appears to have a gas pipe on the right of the lamp over the gate, but gas did not come to Westbury until 1872.

THESE MULTI-PICTURE POSTCARDS provide a reminder of some of the Westbury views and cues for the correction of more past errors.

THE FOUR MAIN CAPTIONS are less than helpful. Top left is Edward Street; top right, Chalford; bottom left, The Laverton; and bottom right, Market Square. Edward Street errors are: Vol. 1, p. 79 – letters from Abraham Laverton in 1869 show that the Lloyds Bank building was formerly a branch of the Wilts. and Dorset Banking Co.; p. 102 – the displaced 'Vineyards' was in Edward Street and bought by Harry Taylor in 1916 as the site for his garage, Taylor's Motors, which became Taylor Bros. when Alf and Fred joined him; p. 77 – previously he had bought J. Martingale's cycle shop in 1913; p. 85 – p. 72 states that the present post office at the bottom end of Edward Street is on the site of the original one. It is, in fact, 20 yds up the road.

THIS POSTCARD was sent in 1908 with a summary of Westbury: 'It is a fine place down here but pretty quiet.' Top left shows the old Leighton Park bridge across the Warminster Road. In Vol. 1, p. 115, the picture is captioned 'Leighton Park showing house and lodge'. Please amend 'lodge' to read 'boat house'.

THE LOPES ARMS and Cannon Green house before they were painted white. The hotel at the time of writing is being cleaned back to the original attractive brickwork. The inn in past centuries was the St George and Dragon and the Earl of Abingdon, before changing allegiance to the new Lord of the Manor to become the Lopes Arms.

JACKSON'S BUTCHER'S SHOP in West End next to the Wheatsheaf pub in 1904. They were both owned by Henry Charles Jackson, a master butcher at 21, born 1864 died 1926. The Wheatsheaf was later badly damaged by fire. In front, with dates of birth in brackets, are: -?-, Maud (1885), Rose (1887), Gladys (1898), mother of Mrs Davies now living in Trowbridge, and Sarah Jackson (1864). The site of the shop is readily identifiable by the tiled canopy. I mistakenly positioned S. Brown's shop here in Vol. 1, p. 42 which was, in fact, on the other side of the road. The new shop was opposite.

THE FORD VAN belonging to Mr J. Hale, about to go on the weighbridge in the Market Place. The dairy was at 60 Warminster Road, where the Oval Garage now is. Mr J. Hale was the grandfather of Mr R.H. Hale of Church Street while his father, Reginald Hale, was the man with the cycle in Vol. 1, p. 110, though not on p. 82, so my guess was wrong.

A DETAIL from a memorial window to Abraham Laverton in the north transept of All Saint's Church. W.H. Laverton, who carried on the cloth business from 1880, was Abraham's nephew, not son as stated in Vol. 1, pp. 8, 57 and 86.

CLAIMED TO BE THE FINEST ENGINE in the county, the 60 hp beam engine operated in Bitham Mill from 1829 to 1939. The factory whistle shown in Vol. 1, p. 61 belonged to Bitham, not Angel Mill, I am told.

A NEW TRUCK for the Westbury Mills in the yard of the Warminster Motor Co.

AT WORK IN ANGEL MILL not long before its closure in 1967. The chimney and unlisted additions to the original building have been demolished this year (1989). The products of the Laverton Mills were awarded a gold medal at the London Exhibition of 1862 and silver in Paris in 1867 for 'very superior fancy coatings in great variety'.

WOMEN'S VOLUNTARY FIRE SERVICE in the Second World War. Front row: Della Reed, Joan Button, Lilian Rogers, Gladys Wheeler. Back row: Audrey Bates, Joan Scott, Betty Wheeler.

THE WAR MEMORIAL in the churchyard being unveiled by Field Marshal Lord Methuen on 17 July 1921. This is still in the same place.

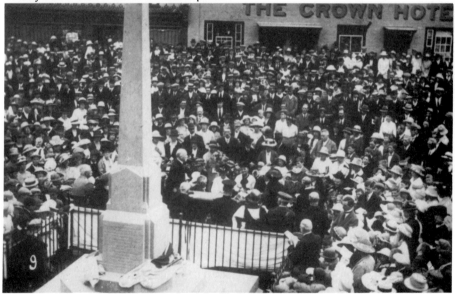

THE TOWN MEMORIAL has since gone from the Market Place and a small memorial to the dead of both world wars is in Soisy Gardens by the library (which used to be Westbury House). Mr W.H. Laverton is speaking to the assembled crowd.

Station Road, Westbury.

HEADING OUT NORTH-WEST towards the railway we take Station Road, here with the milkman and roadman in evidence.

WORKERS AT THE CHEDLET FACTORY on The Ham, in the old RAF hangars there. Continuing on from Station Road down Storridge Road, past the factory, the farm on the left is the much disputed proposed site for the new prison.

WESTBURY STATION AND IRONWORKS in broad gauge days. The Brunel station canopy is evident. The Great Western opted to change to the 'standard' 4 ft 8½ in gauge in 1871 but it took many years to effect throughout the system.

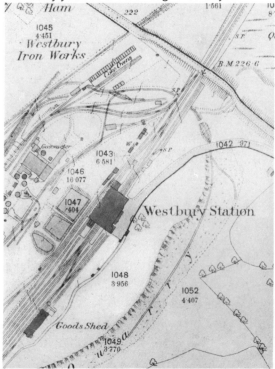

A TRACK PLAN of 1887. The London line came in from the top right in 1900 when the new station was built, and the through line to the west came into operation in 1906.

IN BRITISH RAIL DAYS with Ray Griffiths, driver (in window) and Roy Adams, fireman.

THE FOUR-ROAD ENGINE SHED AT WESTBURY in the days of steam. The right-hand road is to the maintenance shed. The boiler house outside is to produce hot water for de-scaling the locomotive boilers. The track round the right-hand side leads to the turntable. The water tower and coaling stage are of typical GWR design. The shed was built in 1915 and closed in the 1960s.

WESTBURY LOCO MEN in front of GWR *County Carlow* 4–4–0 locomotive, left to right: Frank Grant, Percy Gardener, Arthur Algar, Harry Whale, Harry Gibbs (foreman), Ernest Whittle, William Eyers, George Tucker, Jimmy Arthurs.

Westbury from Railway Station.   Publ. by R. Wilkinson & Cº, Trowbridge.

FROM THE STATION, across the wooded landscape of Westbury in 1905, to the White Horse. Even the minehole lake opposite the Railway Inn, a delightful spot to watch waterfowl, to fish, or to sail, is under threat of partial filling in for a road to come in from yet more urban sprawl to the already congested Station Road.

FROM THE STATION we can go along The Ham and turn off down Shallow Wagon Lane to Heywood with its fine Jacobean-style house, built in 1837 but preserving within it features from the earlier eighteenth-century house.

IN THE 1930s, Mr Sydney Barnes bought the house and carried out much-needed repairs. Here is the hall and through the arch is a finely balustraded staircase.

THE DRAWING ROOM in the early 1960s. The National Trust bought the house in 1982 for use as offices but the ground floor rooms are used for meetings and conferences.

THE WESTBURY UNITED FOOTBALL CLUB has been active for many years. This is one of the earliest photographs of the first team and committee in 1902–3 and is titled Westbury 'Red, White and Blue'. Back row: H. Cadby, T. Cockell, W. Mead (Vice-Captain), Revd. A.J. Kitson, C. Maslin, F.I. Burgess. Centre: S. Smith, W. Scott, F. Golledge (Captain), H. Cox, J. Perrett, A. Hazel (Hon. Sec.), his head is missing from the damaged photograph. Front row: W. Burgess, H. Cornish, G. Collier, T. Richards (Hon. Treas.), F. Smith.

SADLY THERE IS NO PHOTOGRAPH of the notable cricket match in May 1890 between W.H. Laverton's XI (including Dr W.G. Grace) and the Australians, when the Australians were convincingly beaten! However, this picture of cricketers in the 1880s is of interest though I do not know who they are or from which village they come. Vol. 1, p. 111 wrongly suggests that the Australian match was played on the Leighton ground: it had not been laid, nor was the match an annual fixture. We might even see another Laverton XI play in 1990 to celebrate the centenary of the cricket club!

Westbury Leigh

We are still on the trodden path of the earlier book, for Westbury Leigh is still within the parish of Westbury with the church of the Holy Saviour built in 1880 as a chapel of ease. The tower, added in 1890 as a memorial to Richard Phipps, was paid for by his widow. In 1989 repairs to the tower cost £24,000.

Baptist meetings were held in the house of the Phipps family in the seventeenth century until the congregation moved to a barn on the site of the present chapel. In the 1670s, members from this congregation preached in Bratton and in 1720 John Watts left to become minister at Erlestoke, as well as preaching at the Whitaker's house in Bratton.

The name of Phipps recurs in the ownership of mills in the sixteenth and seventeenth centuries and of property up to the twentieth century from Erlestoke Park, Heywood House, Leighton House to Chalcot House, to name only the principal houses. In the Phipps Arms at least the name lives on in Westbury Leigh.

'A suburb of Westbury' is hardly a fair description of Westbury Leigh, though it is sometimes used in publications. With its own industrial base of mills, tannery, malting houses and glove-making, together with substantial Georgian clothiers' houses it grew up more as a self-contained extension of Westbury. It also shared in the approbrium of having 'rough, turbulent people' in 1748.

Whatever its description, let us take another wander down the length of the main street before venturing on to newer 'pastures'.

A 1989 VIEW of Westbury Leigh looking east. Say farewell to the fields on the left, scheduled to be covered by another housing development.

Westbury Leigh.   Westbury Leigh Church.   Glove Factory.

GREETINGS FROM WESTBURY LEIGH

Christmas Greetings

A TIMELY GREETING from Westbury Leigh to match the publication date of the book. Most of the pictures are reminders of some of those published in Vol. 1.

LOOKING TOWARDS THE RAILWAY BRIDGE at Tower Hill.

WESTBURY LEIGH BAPTIST CHURCH was built in 1796 on the site of a barn used for the meetings previously. This church also split, but for a different reason to the Westbury Congregationalists. In 1810 the pastor, George Phillips, and some of the congregation left to form Penknap because of his suspected Wesleyan leanings. Nonconformity was brought to Westbury Leigh in 1672 from Southwick.

THE TANNERY AT WESTBURY LEIGH. The main building is one of two built about 1800 when the mill was known as Boyers Mill, built for the manufacture of cloth. It was bought by Case and Sons around 1900 for leather-dressing and tanning. There was a mill called Woollers on this site, or nearby, in the eighteenth century.

A 1936 VIEW from the west side of the bridge at Tower Hill. Penknap chapel is behind the bridge and the tannery chimney beyond.

THE STAFF AT THE TANNERY.

LEIGH MILL on the Biss south of Boyers Mill in the 1870s. It had been converted to a corn mill just before 1850.

THE CUTTING ROOM of Boulton Bros (Glovers) Ltd. in 1928/9. Bull's mill became a glove factory in 1905 and continued in business until 1969. It had been one of the earliest carding mills in the eighteenth century. The last clothier to use it died in 1830 when it was converted to a corn mill. Some writers refer to this site as Ball's Mill but there may be some confusion as there was a Ball's Water Mill south of and near to Leighton House belonging to T.H.H. Phipps. No mention is made of it after 1811.

Those in the front two rows, left to right, are: Mead (facing inwards) Dance, Shepherd, Collins (foreman – with waistcoat), Simms, Shepherd, Smith, Elkins (with glasses in foreground), Reg Porter, Nunn, Hacker, -?-, Deacon, Shepherd. In the background: Blake, Weston, Blake, White, Simms, Elkins, Porter, Webb, Hacker, Locke, Shepherd, Barber, Pearce, Shepherd, Bowen, Collins. The Shepherd family seem to be firmly established in the glove business!

AT 79 WESTBURY LEIGH, Mr Scott served Westbury Leigh at his grocery shop for 55 years from before the First World War until his death, aged 79. The right-hand part of the shop was for drapery. I tried enlarging and intensifying the poster Mr Scott is pointing to but the definition of the original print was poor, though it would be reasonable to guess it is about 'Vim'! His two daughters live in Westbury.

H.F. BARBER'S SHOP AND BAKERY.

LOOKING TOWARDS LEIGHTON HOUSE in the distance. Scott's shop on the left is not the same shop as Scott's on the previous page, which was on the other side of the road, further towards Dilton Marsh.

COWS STROLLING THROUGH WESTBURY LEIGH. Their lifespan would be brief if they tried it today with the procession of heavy lorries along the narrow street.

THE INHABITANTS of the terraced houses at Penleigh turn out for the photographer.

Dilton Marsh

A distinction no other village in the book shares is a poem to it by John Betjeman. In 'Dilton Marsh Halt' he accurately describes the tiny station in one line: 'There isn't a porter. The platform is made of sleepers.'

The Halt is still there though I did hear of a case where the driver of a train from Salisbury forgot to halt and a taxi had to be provided to take two ladies back home from Westbury!

Having heard Westbury described as 'a really rotten place' with its 'rough ... turbulent people', Dilton Marsh must be quite pleased to get away with its entry in a well-known guide-book on Wiltshire, beginning: 'Dilton Marsh is rather dull ...'!

In 1894 when the civil parish was created out of the western part of Westbury, it extended from the River Biss in the east to the Somerset border in the west and included the north side of Chapmanslade, until 1934. The land is generally low-lying, as 'Marsh' would suggest, with the higher Black Dog Woods rising to the south-west. Chalcot House and Park also lies in the parish and therefore the picture of the house, strictly, should not have appeared in Vol. 1. Likewise, the strip between the Biss and the railway is generally thought of as part of Westbury Leigh.

Even without the portion east of the railway, the village is a full mile long, generally astride the 'B' road one takes when heading for Bath via Beckington. Apart from recent development, most houses date from the eighteenth and nineteenth centuries, many set back from the road on their own plots of land.

The cloth industry had much to do with the expansion of the village but differed from other villages in the area as there were no mills and the work was done on hand looms in the cottages for the clothiers of Warminster and Westbury. This was particularly so in Stormore, or St Maur Common, the south-western loop off the main street. The mechanization of the industry led to poverty and unemployment among the weavers. A number of them marched to Warminster in 1817 with cloth from the looms to protest at the low wages. Soon after, the unemployed were set to work as labourers.

Near Westbury Leigh, houses were built (late nineteenth–early twentieth centuries) for the workers at the tannery there.

Baptist meetings were held for six months in 1810 in a farmyard in Dilton Marsh after George Phillips left the Westbury Leigh Chapel, until the Providence Chapel was built at Penknap. The Baptists at the Stormore end had been meeting in a cottage and the loft of a carpenter's shop but built their own chapel, known as Scott's Meeting, in 1829. It was situated by the same stream used by Westbury Leigh and Penknap for their baptisms. It was rebuilt in 1884 as the mission church of Westbury Leigh and remained so.

The building of the Church of the Holy Trinity was not begun until 1844 and is a fine essay in the late Norman style by T.H. Wyatt.

EVEN A WIDE-ANGLE SHOT shows only about one third of Dilton Marsh. This central section, taken from Black Dog Woods in September 1989, covers the church, on the right, to the beginning of Stormore, on the left.

A POSTCARD POSTMARKED 1920. The views are of a much earlier date with the War Memorial recently added.

CHILDREN at the road junction, c. 1905. The road to Old Dilton on the right is The Hollow.

UNVEILING the First World War Memorial.

THE LADY WITH THE PERAMBULATOR is Mrs Tucker. James Price is in the dark suit and Edwin Garratt with stick.

FROM THE CHURCH TOWER AT A LATER DATE. The roadside trees have gone and there are signs of development. The three-storey house on the left is a weaving master's house, built c. 1830 with workshop behind and four weavers' cottages adjoining.

Dilton Marsh Church.

THE REVERSE VIEW from the picture opposite, c. 1900. The signpost has not yet been erected. The building of Holy Trinity church began in 1844. It was designed by T.H. Wyatt and was largely paid for by T.H.H. Phipps. The south-west portion of the parish of Westbury was assigned to the church in 1845.

Dilton Marsh

THE SAME PICTURE as in the 1920 multi-view postcard, but this delightfully tinted card was postmarked 1907. It is of The Hollow leading from the church up to the Westbury Leigh-Chapmanslade road and across it to Old Dilton.

AT THE WESTBURY LEIGH END of the village, Jim and Julia Pimm stand outside 35 Petticoat Lane after their marriage. Grandpa Millard is seated on the left and the girls in the front are: the now, Mrs Nellie Shell, and Winnie Millard.

CHILDREN AND STAFF of the Church of England School, Dilton Marsh, in 1921 outside the church. This is Class II.

GREETINGS *from* DILTON MARSH

HIGH STREET.

HOLY TRINITY CHURCH

OLD DILTON CHURCH.

WAR MEMORIAL.

IN THE BOTTOM RIGHT PICTURE there are now houses where the orchard was behind the War Memorial in the earlier photographs.

THIS POSTCARD is titled St Mary's Road, whereas the same shop is in the High Street in the top picture.

Dilton Marsh.

LOOKING EAST down the main street.

THE KINGS ARMS.

IF THIS IS THE SHEPHERD FAMILY outside their shop, perhaps some of the young boys are among the five Shepherds in the glove factory in Westbury Leigh.

THE SHOP, with donkey cart for deliveries.

STAN CROOK working on Jim Bull's Farm.   LADIES outside their cottage.

THE ARP IN DILTON MARSH during the Second World War. My military eye notices a certain waywardness in the manner the berets are worn!

STORMORE, the western third of Dilton Marsh, is a continuation to the left of the other 1989 photograph on p. 130.

STORMORE; the Will's Gold Flake advertisements remind me of cigarette card collecting in my schooldays.

STORMORE, looking east.

MR TOM DREDGE, seated with concertina, outside 11 Stormore (it is now No. 26). He was the local barber and took a stool around with him on which he sat to cut hair as he could not stand properly. His housekeeper, Miss Carr pushed him in a wheelchair.

SECTION NINE

Dilton

Leaving Dilton Marsh by The Hollow we climb up to Hisomely between tree-covered banks. Crossing the Westbury–Frome road, the narrow road drops down to the Biss Brook near its source. Tucked discreetly in the steep-sided valley is Dilton, signposted today as Old Dilton, and consisting of a farm, the disused (except for two services a year) but well-kept Church of St Mary and a few cottages.

Not enough to warrant a section of its own, you may be thinking. Admittedly the section is a small one but Dilton for centuries was more important than Dilton Marsh and not connected in any way to it, so it deserves a spot of individual attention. In Vol. I it gained brief mention as a far-flung outpost of Westbury; however, by the beginning of the nineteenth century Dilton Marsh had taken off as a thriving weaving town in its own right and Dilton became 'Old'.

No origin of the name is offered though various spellings have been tried from Dulinton in the twelfth century through Dultun, Dolton, Dilton, Dylton and Delton and back to Dilton. There is an old, small, delightfully simple, church with rubble walls plastered over. The structure is probably fourteenth century with additions up to the eighteenth. Since then there has been hardly any change, with the interior furnishings intact. An eighteenth-century clockmaker of high quality from Warminster, Edward Cockey, made the internal clock, with an octagonal wooden face, for the church.

Despite being so close to the source of the Biss Brook, Dilton too had its mills, Upper and Lower, but only information of the highest on the stream is known and a photograph is included.

A VIEW OF DILTON from the railway embankment in August 1989. The Biss Brook runs round from the left in the steep-sided valley where the few houses are.

THE UPPER MILL AT DILTON was built a little way above the church in the 1790s by the Trowbridge clothier John Waldron. It was the highest mill on the Biss which rises only a short distance away. It was empty in the 1820s and converted to a sawmill, c. 1845.

A 1907 POSTCARD of the Church of St Mary, closed since 1900. The interior, with its bleached box pews and three-decker pulpit is as it was in Georgian times.

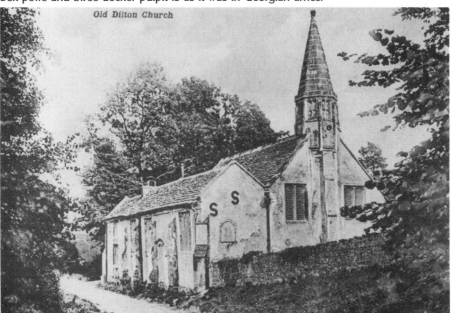

Old Dilton Church

THERE WAS A CHAPLAIN OF DILTON in the thirteenth century and a chapel to St Nicholas recorded in 1362. The structure of St Mary's goes back to these times.

THE ROAD, just visible, is metalled and wider but this peaceful setting is little changed over the years. This photograph was taken in 1982.

ST MARY'S remained a chapelry of Westbury parish throughout its life. Twice a year services are still held, harvest thanksgiving and an advent carol service, conducted by the Vicar of All Saints. This candlelit Advent service would have looked much the same at any time over the last 200 years rather than the 1980s – except perhaps for the 1980s styling of the Revd Michael Flight's glasses!

Upton Scudamore

From Dilton we can take the old lane south-westwards and come into Upton Scudamore on the road from the west, or go eastwards to join the Westbury–Warminster road and approach the village from the toll-house. To appreciate fully that Upton ('Opetone' in Domesday) means 'higher farm' take the direct route on the footpath to Biss Bottom and up the lane. A highwayman named Biss, from Biss, was hanged at Salisbury in 1695.

The Escudamor/Skydemore (the spellings are legion) family held the manor from the Conquest to 1382 when Sir Peter, the last of the male line, died; hence the suffix. Two hundred years ago the village was Skidmores Upton. Two effigies from the thirteenth and fourteenth centuries are in the church, one being of Sir Peter.

Long before the 'Squydemors', early settlers, found the fertile site to their liking after living on the chalk downs. Early Iron and Bronze age artefacts have been found and evidence of a Romano–British settlement.

The Scudamore manor house had long gone when Leland visited in the sixteenth century but he saw the foundations of a 'considerable mansion'. This site is considered to be west of the church, buried beneath farm buildings.

The attractive Manor Farm House was not the manorial farm nor the manor house, but has its origins in Parkescourt of the fifteenth century. The de Parco family held one third of Upton Scudamore for the annual rent of forty shillings and one rose; a delightful touch.

St Mary's Church has a fine Norman font and there are other remains of the early church. It developed over the centuries and was extensively rebuilt in 1750 but by the mid-nineteenth century was described as 'an offensive charnel house' with 'all sorts of deformities and material obstructions to worship'! Under the directions of G.E. Street the church was restored in a more consistent Early English style.

The rector at the time, John Baron, was left with insufficient funds to buy an organ and so designed a compact, economy model with one manual and no pedals. Nelson Hall, an organ-builder, lived in the village and built the organ. Its small size and cheapness made other churches want one too so Nelson Hall moved to Warminster to meet the demand. Later Scudamore organs, as they were known, were built by the celebrated London builder Henry Willis, and many were exported, several to embassies.

Only one nonconformist chapel was built here and that was in 1850 for the Baptists. It was not used after 1907 and was later converted into a house.

The ridge from which extensive views are afforded has the distinction of being the watershed between the Salisbury and Bristol Avons.

UPTON SCUDAMORE in September 1989 from Upton Cow Down. It is not apparent, looking down, that the village lies along a prominent ridge. The tree-lined road below is the A350 (Westbury–Warminster). 'Halfway House' is on the left of the picture with its eighteenth-century octagonal toll-house on the then turnpiked road.

THE HILLTOP LOCATION is not very noticeable in this view either, to the north-west from the north side of Cradle Hill. The new Warminster bypass goes off to the left from the T-junction with the old road in the centre of the picture.

ONE OBTAINS AN UNOBSTRUCTED VIEW, of the attractive Church of St Mary from the south. This photograph was taken in 1980.

COMPARE THIS 1926 NEWSPAPER PICTURE of the church with the one above. The little bell tower was removed in 1951.

THIS WATER TOWER AND WIND PUMP was erected on the east side of the village as a memorial to the Revd Dr John Baron in 1906. The wind pump was later removed when the tank was supplied from the water board's pumping station in Biss Bottom.

PARTS OF THE ORIGINAL NORMAN CHURCH remain with additions and alterations in the thirteenth, fourteenth and fifteenth centuries. The tower and much else was rebuilt c. 1750 and extensive restoration and re-modelling in the 'Early English' style took place in the mid-nineteenth century.

AMATEUR DRAMATICS: Betty Scroggin is played by Frank Muggs; Anna Maria Muffin by Victor G?; the Magistrate by Revd Powley and Mrs Grundy by Jack Greenland.

TEMPLE'S FARM HOUSE was the manorial farm let to the Temple family in 1662 then bought by Peter Temple in 1689, though the manorial rights had lapsed. The house dates from that period, though extensive alterations were made in the nineteenth century.

THIS THATCHED FARMHOUSE is Keyford, on the bend in the road opposite Temple Farm House.

GROUP OUTSIDE THEIR COTTAGES in Upton Scudamore.

ANNIE HARRIET BLAKE was born and bred in Upton Scudamore. In the First World War she became a munitions worker at Uplees Marshes in Faversham, Kent.

THE RAILWAY from Westbury to Warminster and Salisbury was opened in 1851 and passed just to the west of Upton Scudamore in a cutting. The gradients on this line are severe and at this point are the steepest allowed by Brunel.

FRED SHERGOLD driving cows past the water tower towards the main road.

WORKERS IN THE FIELDS with the village behind.

SYDNEY NOAKES.

THE LITTLE GIRL is Rosemary (née Shergold) Adlam.

THE OLD ROADS IN THE VILLAGE do not have names. These three cottages were 12, 13 and 14 Upton Scudamore (now renovated and extended into two houses, Nos. 13 and 14).

I AM HOPING Upton Scudamore will not mind offering a temporary home to this shepherd and his wife, as their names and origin are not known, but it is too good a picture to leave out. The photographer's original retouching is more plain to see than he intended, as the photograph has faded considerably while the retouching has not.

Chapmanslade

The Old English origin of the name, meaning 'the slaed or flat valley of the chapmen or merchants', seems at variance with the position of the village on the highest chunk of land!

Leaving aside the valley on the hill, the next problem was to sort out the history of the parish, for before 1934, when the civil parish was created, all the south side of the village street was in Corsley, and after 1894, when Dilton Marsh was carved out from Westbury, the north side lay in that parish. Other land to the south lay in the parish of Upton Scudamore. Even the soil is divided – light fertile greensand to the east, and to the west, heavier clays.

From Upton Scudamore we can most easily reach Chapmanslade by taking the lane to Thoulstone, which in the early eighteenth century was the main road from Salisbury to Frome and Bath, joining the Westbury–Frome road at Dead Maid's Corner – hardly a name to inspire the traveller. At this point I too had my doubts and wondered whether I was attempting a 'village too far'! I had had very little success in finding old photographs of the village and so felt I should not have strayed so far from the scarp of the Plain. Perhaps the publishers might like to enlarge the area on their chart for future books on the Somerset side to include Chapmanslade, so allowing someone else to have a go, in the hope of giving the coverage the village deserves.

Let us forget the anomalies and leave the dread corner behind to look at the village itself. It is nearly a mile long, spread along the Westbury–Frome road, roughly in the centre of the present parish. In the mainly eighteenth- and nineteenth-century buildings, their links with the weaving industry are evident. The Baptist and Congregational chapels were built on the north side, as was the Church of St Philip and St James, built in 1867 by G.E. Street as a chapel of ease for Dilton Marsh, but transferred to Corsley in 1924.

Visiting Baptist preachers came to Chapmanslade in the late eighteenth century and the minister from Westbury Leigh held regular services in a weaving workshop from 1788 until 1799 when the Baptists built their own church. Richard Parsons from Chapmanslade revived the Baptist church in Corsley and a chapel was built in 1811. To raise the cost of £700 he visited neighbouring towns, Bristol and London, walking all the way and travelling up to 40 miles a day for weeks on end.

The Congregationalists formed their church earlier, in 1761, meeting at first in a barn. They built their own chapel in 1771. A disagreement with the minister in the mid-nineteenth century resulted in a total walk-out of the congregation to join the Baptists down the road. The chapel was pulled down and a new one in stone was built in 1867.

At the western end of the village at Lodge Hill, the highest point, we reach the Somerset border and there I will leave you in the hope you will retrace our steps at leisure over the sections that interest you most and find out about all that I have missed. If you already have, then please ensure your knowledge is passed on.

WITH THE SHORTAGE OF MATERIAL from Chapmanslade I was fortunate to obtain this postcard with seven pictures on it.

THIS SHOWS THE LONG MAIN STREET to advantage, with the road to Corsley dropping away off the ridge to the left. This picture is earlier than the similar view opposite as there is no telephone box or telegraph posts.

DEDICATION OF the First World War Memorial in the churchyard of St Philip and St James Church, built in 1867.

CHAPMANSLADE FOOTBALL CLUB, 1928–9. Back row: W. Neale, C. Bull, Joe Rich, -?- Brown, E. Wilcox, A. Burville. Centre: E. Guy, E. Parfitt, G. Dredge, H. Neale, J. Remyard, V. Merritt, J. Jones, Les Harrison. Front: C. Dunning, R. Crocker, F. Smith, M. Neale, G. Webb.

ACKNOWLEDGEMENTS

How fortunate I have been again in the help so willingly given in putting this book together. Photographs and postcards have been lent for copying without stint, information freely given together with encouragement. I thank everyone for their contributions and the pleasure I have gained from my quest.

I can only hope the welter of facts and names have, in some miraculous way, found their way back from my brain and notes to the right photograph in the right village. If they have not, I apologize, and to those whose pictures I have had to leave out, I can only say it was painful indeed not to include everything.

Some sort of rough balance of content I hope has resulted from the uneven distribution of pictures I had to work with. I am sadly aware of the lack of justice done to some places.

There are people who are acknowledged to be mines of information on their villages who I had hoped to consult, but as time ran desperately short dared not do so for fear of submerging in depths of knowledge from which I would have difficulty in resurfacing. From them I ask their indulgence in what must appear to be a very superficial text but then this has few pretentions beyond being a nostalgic picture book.

At this point I must name names in dread of leaving one out. They are in alphabetical order:

Mr Alan Andrew and all the people whose pictures he has copied
Mrs G. Archer-Smith • Mrs Batchard • Mrs W. Binns • Mrs J. Blakely
Mrs D.M.A. Bright • Miss Norah Bull • Mr J.R. Collins • Mrs Carpenter
Revd Liz Cross • Messrs M. Dyer, L.J. Elkins, Jack Field and the Warminster
History Society • John French • Ray Griffiths • Dick Hale • Robert H. Hale
Mrs A.M. Hannaford • Mrs R.B. Ingram • Messrs G.W.W. Laverton and
E. Manasseh • Mrs Morley • Mrs Pimm • Mr Basil Poffley
Miss Kathleen Reeves • Mrs Shergold • Miss Marjory Taylor • Mrs E.M. Veal
Messrs Bruce Watkin and John Webb • Mrs Williams • Major Robin Wilson

IT SEEMS A PITY to leave a blank page when there is a train picture I could not previously fit in, particularly as the gable end of my house is just visible over the smoke. The train is approaching Westbury station from the Trowbridge–Bristol line and the London line comes in from the right. It was during the excavations here for the railway, c. 1840, that iron was rediscovered on The Ham and artefacts of a Romano-British settlement were found.

TAILPIECE

Among a bundle of photographs and documents lent to me was a letter sent to the Vicar of Dilton Marsh in which I like this sentence: 'If the Departed Verger of Holy Trinity is still hanging in the Choir Vestry, I am his daughter.'